The Magic School Bus
Inside the
Earth

The Magic School Bus
Inside the Earth

By Joanna Cole   Illustrated by Bruce Degen

Hippo

The author and illustrator wish to thank Dr George E Harlow, Associate Curator, Department of Mineral Sciences at the American Museum of Natural History, for his assistance in preparing this book.

The author would also like to thank Dr Peter Bower, Professor of Geology at Barnard College, for his helpful consultation.

Scholastic Children's Books,
Commonwealth House, 1-19 New Oxford Street,
London WC1A 1NU, UK
A division of Scholastic Ltd
London ~ New York ~ Toronto ~ Sydney ~ Auckland

First published in the US by Scholastic Inc.
This edition published by Scholastic Ltd, 1996

In Miss Frizzle's class,
we had been learning about
animals' homes
for almost a month.
We were pretty tired of it.
So everyone was happy
when Miss Frizzle announced,
"Today we start something new."

SOMETHING NEW.
THANK GOODNESS!

GET OFF!

Beaver Lodge

PRAIRIE DOG
TOWN

"We are going to study
our Earth!" said Miss Frizzle.
She put us to work
writing reports on what
we knew about Earth science.
"And for homework,"
she said,
"each person must find a rock
and bring it to school."

But the next day, almost everyone had some excuse.

I COULDN'T FIND ANY ROCKS.

I FOUND ONE, BUT MY DOG ATE IT.

YOUR DOG ATE A ROCK?

WHERE DO ROCKS COME FROM?
by Wanda

Most of the solid part of the Earth is made of great masses of rock.

The small rocks that we collect are just pieces that broke off from these huge masses.

9

Only four people
had done the homework.
And Phil was the only one
who had found a real rock.

THAT'S NOT A ROCK!

IT IS TOO A ROCK!

IT'S PART OF AN OLD 7-UP BOTTLE.

YOU CHIPPED THIS OFF THE PAVEMENT, DIDN'T YOU, WANDA?

MY ROCK
ALEX

MY ROCK
QUARTZITE
PHIL

"I suppose we'll have to go on a field trip and collect rocks." said Miss Frizzle.

WHAT ARE ROCKS MADE OF?
by Tim
Rocks are made of minerals. Sometimes you see tiny specks of different colours in a rock. Sometimes you see shiny specks. These different specks are the different minerals that make up the rock.

You never know
what will happen
on a trip with Miss Frizzle.
Her new dress
was a trip in itself.
At first the old school bus
wouldn't start.
But finally we were on our way.

I CAN'T BELIEVE MISS FRIZZLE DRESSES LIKE THAT.

YOU'LL GET USED TO IT.

When we came to the field,
all the kids wanted
to get out of the bus.
But suddenly,
the bus began to spin like a top.
That sort of thing doesn't happen
on most class outings.

THE EARTH'S CRUST
by John

The outside of the Earth is a shell of hard rock and soil. This shell is called the Earth's crust.

THIS CRUST IS AS HARD AS A ROCK, TOO.

When the spinning finally stopped,
some things had changed.
We all had on new clothes.
The bus had turned into
a digger.
And there were shovels and picks
for every kid in the class.
"Start digging!"
yelled Miss Frizzle.
And we began making a huge hole
right in the middle of the field.

THIS ISN'T EXACTLY EASY.

AT LEAST WE'RE MISSING SPELLING.

14

15

Before long – CLUNK! – we hit rock.
The Friz handed out pneumatic drills.
We began to break
through the hard rock.

THERE IS ALWAYS
ROCK UNDER YOU
by Shirley

Most of the rock in the Earth's crust is covered with soil or water. But if you dig deep enough, you will find the rock. Wherever you are standing or walking or floating on Earth...

there is rock under you.

SOIL
ROCK

WATER
ROCK

I'M NOT USED TO MISS FRIZZLE YET!

GIVE IT TIME.

We chipped off pieces of the rocks for our class rock collection. "These rocks are called *sedimentary* rocks, class," said Miss Frizzle. "There are often fossils in sedimentary rocks."

SANDSTONE IS MADE OF GRAINS OF SAND ALL PRESSED TOGETHER.

SHALE IS MADE OF MUD AND CLAY ALL PRESSED TOGETHER.

SANDSTONE FEELS GRAINY.

THIS SHALE HAS A FOSSIL OF A LEAF IN IT.

THIS LIMESTONE HAS A FOSSIL OF A SEASHELL IN IT.

THAT'S BECAUSE LIMESTONE IS MADE OF SHELLS ALL PRESSED TOGETHER.

MILLIONS OF YEARS AGO, THERE WAS A SEA HERE.

WHY THERE ARE FOSSILS IN ROCK LAYERS
by Phoebe

Sometimes a prehistoric plant or animal died and was buried in layers of mud, sand, or crushed shells. Then it turned to rock along with the layers. It became a fossil.

FOSSIL: ARCHEOPTERYX

DINOSAUR EGGS

19

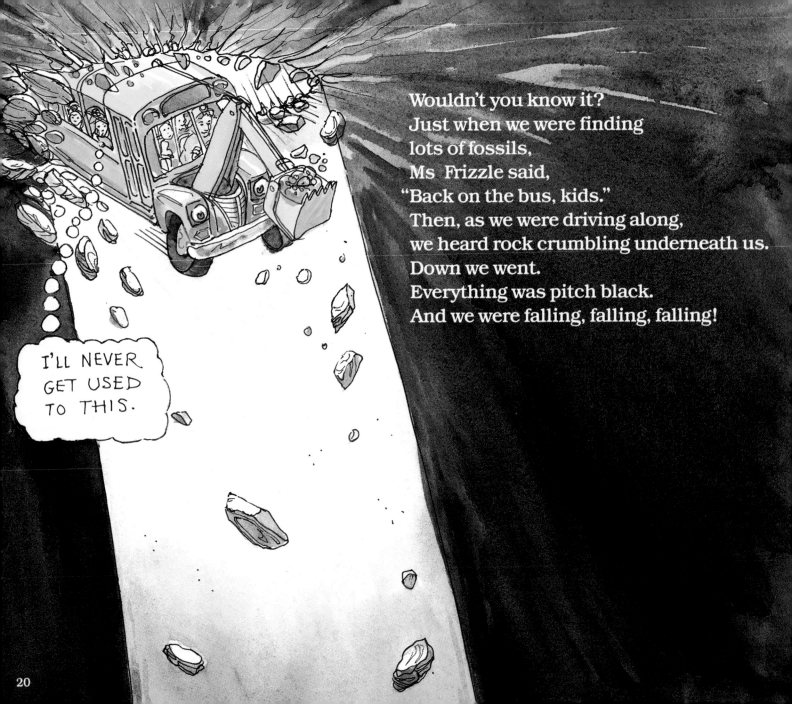

Wouldn't you know it?
Just when we were finding
lots of fossils,
Ms Frizzle said,
"Back on the bus, kids."
Then, as we were driving along,
we heard rock crumbling underneath us.
Down we went.
Everything was pitch black.
And we were falling, falling, falling!

I'LL NEVER GET USED TO THIS.

We landed with a bump.
Miss Frizzle switched on the headlights.
We had fallen through a hole
into a huge limestone cave.
"Rainwater has been dripping down
through the earth for ages,"
said Miss Frizzle.
"The water wore away this cave
in the rock."

THE EMPIRE STATE
BUILDING IS MADE
OF LIMESTONE, TOO.

THIS WHOLE CAVE IS
MADE OF LIMESTONE.
CAN YOU FIND MORE
FOSSILS HERE?

HERE'S ONE,
MISS FRIZZLE.

KNOCK IT OFF!

22

The further down we went,
the hotter it got.
The rocks were harder, too.
"These are rocks that were changed
from one kind to another kind
by heat and pressure,"
explained The Friz.
"Rocks that were changed
are called *metamorphic* rocks."

We had dug all the way
through the Earth's crust.
It was so hot now
that Miss Frizzle told us to
get back in the bus.

She stepped on the accelerator
and the bus started *really* drilling.
Soon we were actually inside the Earth.
It was hot, hot, hot!
And it got hotter and hotter
as we zoomed towards the centre.

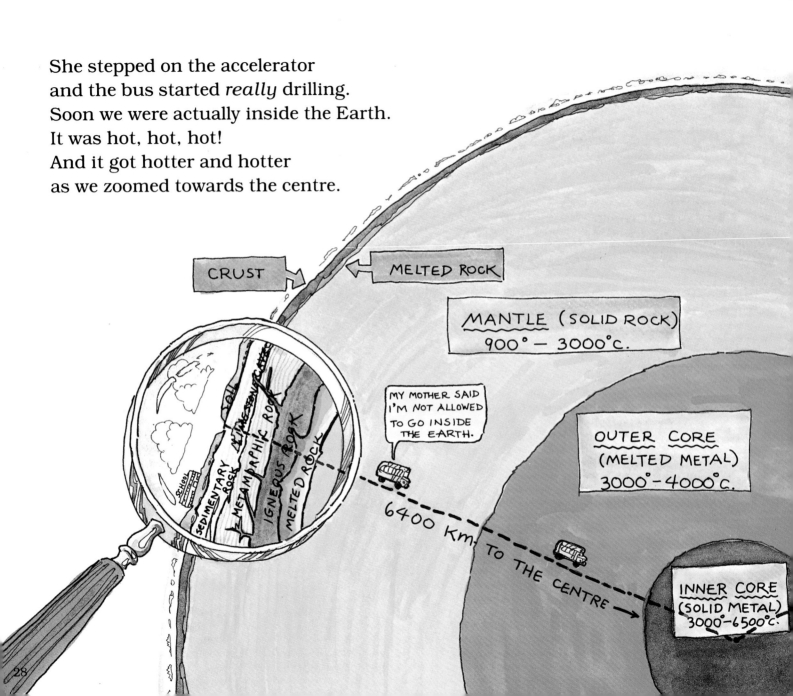

We were glad when Miss Frizzle
headed out again.
We reached the Earth's crust
and drove straight up through
a tunnel of black rock.
It was great to see the sky.

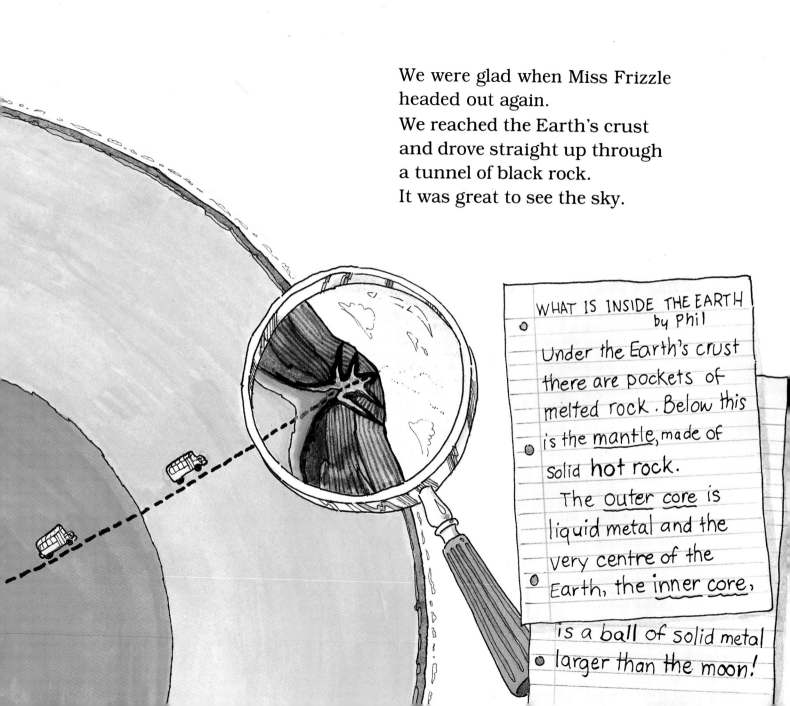

WHAT IS INSIDE THE EARTH
by Phil

Under the Earth's crust
there are pockets of
melted rock. Below this
is the <u>mantle</u>, made of
solid hot rock.
   The <u>outer core</u> is
liquid metal and the
very centre of the
Earth, the <u>inner core</u>,

is a ball of solid metal
larger than the moon!

WHAT IS A VOLCANO?
by Rachel

A volcano is an opening in the Earth's crust where melted rock can flow out.

Volcanoes come in different shapes:

CINDER CONE VOLCANO   COMPOSITE VOLCANO   SHIELD VOLCANO

ARE MISS FRIZZLE AND THE KIDS ON A CINDER CONE, A COMPOSITE VOLCANO, OR A SHIELD VOLCANO?

I WANNA GO HOME!

Then we looked around.
We had come out on an island
in the middle of the ocean!
"Isn't this wonderful, class?"
said Frizzie.
"We've driven right up
on a volcanic island!"
It didn't look like much.
But if Miss Frizzle was right,
the whole island was one big volcano!

We were nervous, but Miss Frizzle made us collect some rocks.
She said they had all hardened from melted rock that had come out of the volcano.
Then, suddenly, we heard rumblings from below.

VOLCANOES MAKE NEW LAND   by Arnold

The material that comes out of a volcano is melted rock called lava. When lava cools, it hardens into new rock. In time, soil forms on the rock and plants can grow.

I DIDN'T KNOW VOLCANOES COULD BE USEFUL!

We scrambled into the bus.
The Friz turned the ignition key
and stepped on the accelerator.
Nothing happened.
The bus would not start!
We thought we were goners!

UH-OH

Red-hot lava came streaming
out of the volcano.
Some of it shot into the air
like a fountain.
Some of it flowed over the land
like a river.
Our bus went along with it —
right into the sea.

33

When the red-hot lava hit the water,
it made a huge cloud of steam.
All we could see was white.
We seemed to be rising
with the steam and floating along.
No one knows how long
we floated in the cloud . . .

but when it finally cleared,
we were back in the school car park.

It had been the strangest field trip, but we *did* get a great rock collection for our classroom.

ARNOLD, THAT'S NOT A ROCK THAT'S POLYSTYRENE.

NOT AGAIN!

Rock COLLECTION

by MISS FRIZZLE'S CLASS

HEY! I'M NOT A ROCK!

SHIRLEY'S ROCK
LIMESTONE

TYPE: Sedimentary (formed from shells)
USES: Buildings, chalk, cement, fertilizer

Amanda Jane's rock
MARBLE

TYPE: Metamorphic (formed from limestone)
USES: Statues, monuments, buildings

Phoebe's rock
SHALE

TYPE: Sedimentary (formed by mud)
USES: Ground up and mixed with limestone for cement, brick

Wanda's rock
GRANITE

TYPE: Igneous
USES: Monuments, buildings, Kerbstones

JOHN'S rock
SLATE

TYPE: Metamorphic (formed from shale)
USES: Roofing tile, flagstones, chalkboards

Michael's rock
SANDSTONE

TYPE: Sedimentary (formed by sand)
USES: Buildings, grindstones

MOLLY'S rock
BASALT
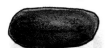
TYPE: Igneous (Volcanic)
USES: Road Building

Rachel's rock
OBSIDIAN

TYPE: Igneous (Volcanic)
USES: Decoration, Indian Arrowheads

Florrie's rock
PUMICE

TYPE: Igneous (Volcanic)
USES: Ground-up in Scouring powder

Phil's rock
QUARTZITE

TYPE: Metamorphic (formed from sandstone)
USES: Millstones for grinding grain, road building

A WORD WITH THE AUTHOR AND THE ARTIST

The first reader of this book called to complain. He said the book was full of mistakes. We recorded the conversation to help you decide which things are true and which were put in to make the story more exciting.

READER: This book is full of mistakes!

AUTHOR: It is not!

ARTIST: Everything in this book is absolutely true and really happened.

READER: What about the beaver lodge on page 7?

AUTHOR: Oh, that. Well, I suppose that *would* be too messy in a real classroom.

READER: And the beehive?

ARTIST: That, too. But everything else is fact.

READER: Oh, come *on!* You mean kids can use pneumatic drills (page 16), and a bus can change into a digger (page 14) and a drill (page 23)?

AUTHOR: Well, er, now that you mention it, that is not really possible.

READER: And do you expect me to believe that a bus can go through the centre of the Earth (page 28)?

ARTIST: Yes . . .

AUTHOR: Maybe . . .

ARTIST: Well, actually, no. The bus couldn't do that, either.

AUTHOR: Even if a bus *could* drill its way through, the distance is so long that the trip would take months, even years.

READER: And what about the heat?

AUTHOR: Okay, okay! It's white-hot in the centre of the Earth. The bus would be burned up in a minute.

READER: Isn't it ridiculous to say that air-conditioning would help?

AUTHOR: Okay, you're right. Air-conditioning could not make any difference in that kind of heat.

READER: And the bus could not flow in lava and go up in a cloud of steam (pages 33–34)?

ARTIST: Give us a break! You're right again. That's not true, either.

READER: But you said *everything* was true!

AUTHOR: Everything *else* is. Honest!

READER: Everything else is true? There truly are sedimentary, metamorphic and igneous rocks?

AUTHOR: Certainly!

READER: And lava really does harden into new rock?

ARTIST: Oh, yes.

READER: And what about Miss Frizzle's clothing?

AUTHOR: That *is* hard to believe, but it's true.

ARTIST: She really does dress that way!

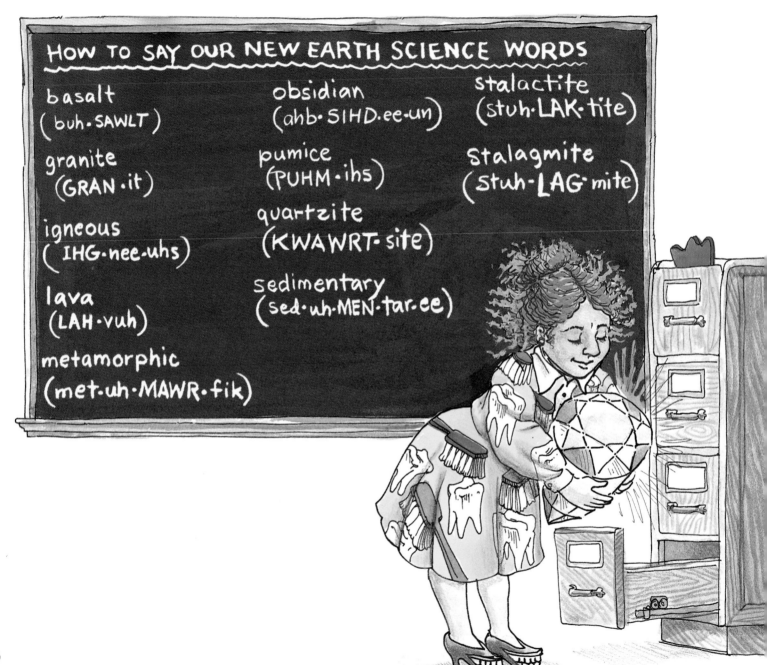

HOW TO SAY OUR NEW EARTH SCIENCE WORDS

basalt
(buh·SAWLT)

granite
(GRAN·it)

igneous
(IHG·nee·uhs)

lava
(LAH·vuh)

metamorphic
(met·uh·MAWR·fik)

obsidian
(ahb·SIHD·ee·un)

pumice
(PUHM·ihs)

quartzite
(KWAWRT·site)

sedimentary
(sed·uh·MEN·tar·ee)

stalactite
(stuh·LAK·tite)

stalagmite
(stuh·LAG·mite)